£2 50
Hallsworth
Howard

DRUG ABUSE:

DRUG ABUSE:

Yours Questions
Answered

LIZ HODGKINSON

WARD LOCK

A WARD LOCK BOOK

First published in the UK 1995
by Ward Lock
Wellington House
125 Strand
LONDON
WC2R OBB

A Cassell Imprint

Distributed in the United States
by Sterling Publishing Co., Inc.
387 Park Avenue South, New York, NY 10016-8810

Distributed in Australia
by Capricorn Link (Australia) Pty Ltd
2/13 Carrington Road, Castle Hill NSW 2154

A British Library Cataloguing in Publication Data block for this book
may be obtained from the British Library

ISBN 0 7063 7400 2
Design and computer make-up by Tony & Penny Mills
Printed and bound in Great Britain by Biddles

Liz Hodgkinson is a journalist and author who has contributed to most leading
publications in the UK, including The Times, Guardian, Independent, Daily Mail, Cosmopolitan, and
Woman's Own. She broadcasts extensively on radio and television, has presented 'Woman's
Hour' and edits the magazine Top Woman. She is the author of more than 25 books on a
variety of subjects.

The information in this book is believed to be accurate at the time of
publication. However, the book is intended purely as a reference and not as
a substitute for medical advice. Anyone who is concerned about their health
should consult a qualified medical practitioner.

Contents

Introduction

Ever since the 1960s, use – or abuse, depending on how you look at it – of psychotropic (mind-altering) drugs for recreational purposes has been seen as an ever-growing problem. The few young-sters who daringly took a few drags of a cannabis joint in the early 1960s have given way to an entire drug culture that has alarmed and terrified those sections of the community which see all drug taking as wicked, immoral and degenerate.

According to the latest statistics, virtually everyone under 25 years old has tried cannabis, and the use of recreational drugs, e.g. ecstasy, LSD (lysergic acid diethylamide) and cocaine, has become a standard feature of the youth dance scene. Whereas, at one time, young people sedately took their partners for a waltz or the Veleta, they are now, or so we are led to believe, stage-diving and bopping all night while crazed on a mixture of drugs, alcohol and ear-splittingly loud music.

Most people who are not, and never have been, part of the drug scene have certain mental pictures and pre-conceptions of what drug taking is like: evil pushers, dark, swarthy drug barons from South America, foisting expensive drugs on to unsuspecting young people, drugs which they have adulterated with even more toxic substances to produce a lethal cocktail; heroin addicts sharing dirty needles, desperately looking for veins and committing increasingly unspeakable crimes to support their increasingly expensive habit; hard-bitten, rich city types, snorting their cocaine as they deal in millions of pounds and dollars across the world; secondary-school children on inner city estates, stealing correction fluid and nail-polish remover to sniff and snort until they get high.

These images are all extremely potent and are fuelled mainly by ignorance and fear. But how accurate are they? Are young people today really all sinking into a drug-crazed lifestyle, alternating between crashing out and being on a drug-induced high? Are heroin addicts really all sad, desperate people? Or does the truth lie somewhere else?

One of the main problems with the kind of drugs which are discussed in this book is that they are illegal and, because of this, people are not supposed to take them, or it sometimes seems, even to know about them. Although, these days, police and courts are turning an increasingly blind eye to so-called soft (or supposedly non-addictive) drugs, the fact remains that supplying, dealing in, and taking cannabis are offences punishable by a fine or a prison sentence. And when hard drugs are involved these measures are almost always imposed.

The questions raised by the taking of recreational drugs are many. Firstly, why are increasing numbers of people taking drugs? Why are some people apparently unable to get enough satisfaction, excitement, arousal, from *legal* substances and activities? Why do they have to turn to something beyond the law? And will everyone who tries illegal drugs get hooked and turn into a hopeless junkie?

The issues are so emotive, and drugs are so strongly condemned, that it can be difficult to sort out fact from fiction. This book is an attempt to present the truth about drugs and drug taking, the dangers and problems, and the various ways of coming off drugs and living a life without them in the belief that nobody can condemn drugs and drug taking unless they know exactly what they are condemning – and why.

We know that drug taking is vastly on the increase. Heroin, which had been used therapeutically as a painkiller for several decades, reached the streets of London, and a few other major UK cities, from the USA during the 1950s.

And throughout the 1960s almost the only people who took heroin illegally in the UK – virtually the only ones who had even heard of it – were those heavily involved in the rock and jazz scene.

In those days, however, heroin addicts were rare indeed, numbering only a few dozen. Now, we are told, there are many thousands of young people, and older ones as well, taking the stuff for kicks.

Why? Those who have never taken, or who have never been tempted, to take an illegal drug, may find this hard to understand. Whereas the attraction of wine, cigarettes and cigars may be easy to appreciate (and their seductive appeal is helped at least partly by advertising) drugs are represented in a totally negative light. Many people in the UK, for example, can remember the Government's 'Heroin Screws You Up' campaign, and the picture which it portrayed of drug takers. Yet a minute's thought would tell us that there must be something attractive about recreational drugs, or nobody would take them at all.

The main point about drugs, at least the kind dealt with in this book, is that they are powerfully mind-altering. Basically, they are of two kinds: stimulants and depressants, or 'uppers' and 'downers' in common parlance. Stimulants intensify the emotions and make the world seem a more colourful and exciting place whereas depressants relieve anxieties. Broadly speaking, cocaine is a stimulant and heroin is a depressant.

Some people, it is true, have no desire to take any mind-altering substance stronger than tea. But if tea addicts try giving up their 'substance' for a fortnight, they will experience withdrawal symptoms in much the same way as an addict coming off drugs. They will grow ever more desperate for a cup of tea. Coffee addicts suffer more because coffee is more addictive than tea. In fact, when anybody says they are 'dying' for a cup of tea or coffee, they are telling you that they are an addict. Anybody who is quick to condemn all drug addicts should keep this in mind. Few people take much notice of tea and coffee addiction however. Both are mild stimulants but they seem harmless enough. After all, few people are caught shoplifting or committing other crimes in order to support a tea and coffee habit!

The reason why recreational drugs exert such a dark fascination is that, because they are illegal, a certain way of life goes with their use. You can be a tea or coffee drinker, a chain smoker or an alcoholic – or all of these – and obtain your substances quite legally at the nearest supermarket. But you cannot obtain recreational drugs without resorting, at least to some extent, to criminal practices. Whatever you may think of the laws governing such drugs, they are illegal in the UK and anyone who uses them is therefore a criminal.

Many people think that there is a direct link between smoking a joint behind the school bicycle sheds and becoming a hopeless junkie, living from one injected fix to the next, and having an arm full of sores and scratches and dying of AIDS. While it is certainly true that in some cases the use of heroin can lead to death, it is also true that some people, albeit not many, have been taking heroin for 25 years or more and are living otherwise relatively normal lives.

Of the tens of thousands of heroin users in the UK, only a few hundred deaths each year are heroin-induced. Where death occurs it tends to result from overdose. Sometimes people mistakenly take a far stronger dose than they are used to. In other cases, people who have given up heroin for a while go back to taking their accustomed dose which can then be too strong for the body to cope with. There are also deaths related to infection passed on by the use of shared, infected needles.

Many talented people have been drug addicts and people with experimental minds have often resorted to drugs to expand their perception. Writers such as Thomas de Quincey, Samuel Taylor Coleridge, Aldous Huxley and Jack Kerouac and some beat poets of the 1950s and 1960s fall into these categories. Nevertheless it should be remembered that drug taking cannot create talent where talent does not exist.

Para

Drug taking is an attempt to deal with life's problems, by adding more excitement, by reducing anxiety or calming nerves, or by making life, in some way, more comfortable or endurable. The curious, the adventurous, those in deep emotional pain or anguish, have always been attracted to psychotropic drugs, the use of which dates back to the beginnings of time and is recorded in virtually every culture.

Drugs are causing concern in our present society because of the increasing numbers of people who are using them. It is because of this that they are no longer a marginal consideration.

This book gives the most up-to-date information on the recreational drugs available, the various treatments for drug addiction and recovery, and the success rates for each. It also tries to answer the vexed question of why some people feel the need to resort to substances which, eventually, may have an extremely destructive influence on their life, health, relationships, career and personality.

Questions
and
Answers

1 Information on Drugs

Q Which drugs are mainly abused?

The main drugs currently used for non-medical, or 'recreational', purposes are categorized below according to their actions.

1. Stimulants: amphetamines (speed, uppers, bennies); methylenedioxyamphetamine (MDMA, ecstasy) – an hallucinogenic amphetamine; cocaine (coke, snow, crack).

2. Depressants: barbiturates (barbs, downers), which include nitrazempan and tetrazepam; benzodiazepines (tranquillizers), e.g. diazepam (Valium); heroin (horse, junk, smack); solvents and gases.

3. Hallucinogens: lysergic acid diethylamide (LSD, acid); cannabis (marijuana, grass, pot).

4. Others: nitrites – amyl and butyl nitrites (poppers); anabolic steroids.

The possession, supply and manufacture of most of these drugs are controlled under the Misuse of Drugs Act 1971 whereby it is illegal to possess them without a prescription or to manufacture and supply them. The Medicines Act 1968 regulates the medicinal use of those drugs which have a medical use. These include some, but by no means all, of the types of drugs listed here.

Q What is the difference between 'using' and 'abusing' an illegal drug?

The difference is really a matter of terminology and depends on one's point of view. The term 'abuse' means 'to use badly', or 'misuse'. People who take drugs such as cocaine, ecstasy and heroin probably consider that they 'use' rather than 'abuse' their substances. On the other hand, people who have never taken illegal drugs, and who regard all such use as immoral and dangerous, are more likely to talk in terms of 'abuse', in a pejorative fashion.

Strictly speaking, abuse occurs when a drug is used in a way, or for a purpose, for which it was not originally intended; e.g. injecting substances formulated for medical use (such as heroin, barbiturates or tranquillizers) in order to get an instant high. Whether or not the term 'abuse' can be applied to drugs such as crack, ecstasy or LSD, whose only known use is recreational, is debatable.

Occasional use of a recreational drug can hardly be termed abuse. If you take cannabis, do you use or abuse it? If you smoke, do you use or abuse cigarettes? Does an alcoholic use or abuse alcohol? Is it a matter of quantity, method of delivery, or choice of drug?

Perhaps 'use' becomes 'abuse' when a person's life has become entirely centred on the drug and he, or she, can no longer exist without taking expensive, illegal and dangerous drugs every day.

The distinction is a difficult one, and is further complicated by the illegality and criminality which surrounds these substances.

Q How harmful are these drugs?

Not all drugs are equally harmful, but much depends on the way in which they are taken, how often and for what purposes, the purity of the supplies, and the general lifestyle of the user. Some people believe that many currently illegal drugs do no more harm than mild stimulants, such as tea, coffee and colas.

The effects depend largely on the individual user's metabolism, health and personality. Some people become tremendously high, and even ill, from one drag on a cannabis joint, while others have no reaction at all. Some authorities believe that, if a well-adjusted, contented person takes heroin, he or she will feel ill and nauseous and not be inclined to repeat the experience, but if someone who feels depressed, alienated or desperately out of touch with themselves and the world in general takes the same amount, they run the risk of wanting to repeat the experience and thus becoming addicted.

Because of the wide variations in individual responses to mind-altering substances, it is difficult to assess how harmful they are. One should also bear in mind that some psychotropic drugs, e.g. sleeping pills, anxiety-reducing drugs and tranquillizers, are regularly prescribed by doctors. Indeed, these medicines, designed to help patients over a 'rough patch', are the most frequently prescribed. The body, also, generates its own mind-altering substances, e.g. adrenaline and sex hormones, all of which can bring about an altered state of consciousness.

The harm, of course, comes when people come to depend on illegal drugs for their very existence, and when their bodies have become so used to regular large shots of the drug that their systems simply cannot do without it. Such dependence affects not just the body but also the mind and perceptions, because, when people are addicted, their lives become narrowed down to a point where their only concern is the next fix of the drug.

Addicts of any kind tend to become devious, sly, manipulative, selfish, uncaring, self-centred, often to an appalling degree, and lose all empathy with those around them. Often, of course, drug users become like this in order to gain access to an illegal substance. The real harm though, perhaps, comes not from the drug itself but for the reasons it is taken.

If the point is to blot everything out and arrive at oblivion, then any drug will become harmful. This applies to coffee, sugar, gambling, alcohol – anything which can be taken to have this effect – quite as much as to drugs which are currently illegal.

Q What is the difference between 'hard' and 'soft' drugs?

The terms 'hard' and 'soft' are references to the relative safety of the drug in question but have no legal or medical validity. They can, in fact, be confusing and unhelpful, perhaps leading people to assume that a drug generally regarded as 'soft' is relatively harmless. For example, ecstasy and LSD may not cause serious harm, but are regarded as Class A drugs along with heroin and cocaine within the UK legal system. All countries have laws regulating drug use although these may vary. In the UK, there are currently two statutes concerning drugs and their legal status.

The Misuse of Drugs Act 1971 is intended to prevent the non-medical use of certain drugs and strongly affects the general public. Drugs subject to this act are known as 'controlled drugs' and include all the illegal substances discussed in this book. They are classed as follows:

Class A: cocaine, heroin, LSD, opium derivatives, ecstasy

Class B: amphetamines, barbiturates, cannabis

Class C: most benzodiazepines

The offences which can be committed for dealing in, or being in possession of these drugs, and the penalties for offenders, are defined in law. Under this Act, the police have the power to stop, search and detain anyone on reasonable suspicion of being in possession of a controlled drug. Penalties and sentences are graded according to the class of drug.

Any Class B drug prepared for injection is treated as a Class A drug because injection is perceived to be the most dangerous method of delivery.

The maximum penalties in the UK can be severe but, in practice, are hardly ever imposed to the full. This, of course, will vary depending on the class of drug and the individual offender. On average, only 20 per cent of offenders receive a custodial sentence and, in 1995, only three-quarters of all fines exceeded £50.

The Medicines Act of 1968, which governs medicinal supply and use, classifies drugs as follows:

1. Available only on prescription.

2. Available without prescription, but only from registered pharmacists.

3. Sold with no restriction, but which must carry certain labels and can only be advertised in a certain way.

Q Are these drugs natural or synthetic?

It depends on the drug. Some, like ecstasy, are completely chemically synthesized, whereas

23

others, such as cannabis, are relatively natural and untouched by chemical processes. Although many illegal drugs may be prepared partly from natural substances, the majority of those available have been prepared in the laboratory.

In addition, street drugs are often adulterated, or 'cut', with non-mind-altering substances, e.g. chalk, flour, bicarbonate of soda, or glucose, to make them go further and increase the dealers' profit margins. Thus a serious problem with street drugs, as opposed to prescription drugs, is that purity of supplies cannot be guaranteed. Although this may make the drug weaker and, therefore, in some ways less 'dangerous', it can be equally dangerous to inject the cutting substance into a vein. Indeed, some people consider that the main harm from street drugs comes not from the drugs themselves but from the substances with which they are adulterated.

Q Most people consider heroin to be the most dangerous of all street drugs. How did it get this reputation?

Heroin is a partly synthetic derivative of the opium poppy and is one of the narcotic drugs. The word 'heroin' was coined in 1898 by Heinrich Dreser, chief pharmacist of the pharmaceutical company Friedrich Bayer and Son and it was first used in a cough mixture. Dreser alleged that heroin was not habit-forming and foresaw it becoming a useful tranquillizing and painkilling medicine.

Along with other opium derivatives, e.g. morphine, codeine, diconal and methadone, it was used as a painkiller, almost entirely by the medical profession, until the 1930s when the first heroin addicts were notified to the British Home Office.

At this time, these addicts were mainly people who had become addicted to prescribed morphine. They numbered less than 200. Since then the non-medical use of heroin has grown and grown and, although it is still used therapeutically in some countries its main outlet nowadays is to heroin addicts. Currently far more people use heroin non-therapeutically than for medicinal reasons.

 What is LSD?

LSD is an hallucinogenic drug with a fearsome reputation, which may not be entirely justified. LSD (lysergic acid diethylamide) is made from ergot, a fungus which grows on rye, and was discovered in 1938. The very first LSD trip was taken in 1943.

In the 1960s, the therapeutic use of the drug became sanctified by psychotherapists as a means of opening up hitherto closed areas of the mind and bringing long-buried fears to the surface where they could be harmlessly dissipated.

Widely used by young people in the 1960s, during the 'flower power' era, it became less popular in the 1970s and 1980s. Today it has returned as an effective drug with which to get stoned at dances and 'raves'.

It is classified as a Class A drug in the UK and carries maximum penalties for misuse.

Q What exactly is ecstasy?

Chemically, ecstasy is known as methylenedioxyamphetamine (MDMA) and, as the name suggests, it is an amphetamine-based drug, first synthesized in 1917. It has the properties of both an hallucinogen and a stimulant, and is technically known as an hallucinogenic amphetamine.

Although it was developed so long ago, no therapeutic use was found for it until the 1960s, when it was used in the treatment of marital problems because of its ability to produce temporary empathy between people. This effect, however, lasts only as long as the drug. Once its properties became known, it leaked out into the drug-taking population, but it was hardly known until the mid-1980s. Nowadays, its use is more or less confined to those attending dances and raves, as it endows people with far more energy than they might otherwise have and enables them to dance all night.

Ecstasy is a controlled, Class A drug and nowadays has no known medical use. It is taken in tablet form and has a variety of street names, of which the best known is simply 'E'.

Q Is cannabis dangerous and can it lead to hard drug taking?

In itself, cannabis is not particularly dangerous and it appears to have been taken in some form or other since the dawn of civilization. Whether or not it can lead to hard drug taking is debatable. It is likely that the vast majority of people who have taken cannabis – and nowadays there is hardly anyone under 25 years old who has not tried it – just experiment with the drug for a time, then forget all about it and never go on to harder substances.

The small minority who do progress from cannabis to heroin and cocaine probably would have done so anyway; they may well be the type of people who seek drug-induced highs and lows. In other words, it is probably not the cannabis which is at fault, but the deep-seated need in the user to blot out mental anguish.

Cannabis is derived from *Cannabis sativa*, a plant that grows wild in most parts of the world and can be easily cultivated in the UK. In those parts of the world where it is traditionally used, it acts as a relaxant and mild intoxicant.

The active ingredients are substances chemically known as tetrahydrocannabinoids (THC) and these are concentrated in the resin found at the top of the plants. 'Hash', or hashish, which is the most commonly available form in the UK, is resin taken from the plant and then compressed into blocks. Herbal cannabis, also known as marijuana, is a weaker preparation of the plant material. Sinsemilla, which comes from the flowering top of the unfertilized female plant, is particularly potent. Strongest of all is cannabis oil, which is prepared by percolating a solvent through the resin.

The first documented use of cannabis, which has medical uses in certain chronic or serious illnesses, was as a herbal remedy in the first

Century AD in China. Recreational use of this drug dates back to Ancient China and later became established in India. Non-medical use of cannabis was prohibited in the UK in 1928. In those days it was hardly used at all, but it became popular during the 1960s. It was originally used by immigrant groups, spread to jazz clubs and, from the 1960s onwards, became increasingly a part of youth culture. It was available on prescription in the UK, although little used, until 1973.

Currently, it is controlled under the Misuse of Drugs Act 1971 as a Class B drug and it is illegal in the UK to cultivate, produce, supply or possess the substance.

Campaigns for its legalization have been going on since the 1960s, but have so far fallen on deaf ears. It is the most commonly used of all the currently illegal drugs.

Are barbiturates still popular?

The non-medical use of barbiturates (barbs) grew to notoriety during the 1960s, when they were 'busted' at chemists' shops. Barbiturates are depressant drugs which came into widespread use during the 1950s and 1960s under the brand names of, e.g. Tuinal, Seconal, and Nembutal.

They were widely prescribed as sleeping pills and for the treatment of certain anxiety states.

Prescriptions in the UK fell from over 16 million in 1966 to about 800,000 in 1992, and their use is still falling. They are now hardly used medically, having been superseded by newer drugs less likely to cause death from overdose. They are controlled drugs under Class C of the Misuse of Drugs Act 1971, and it is illegal to produce or supply them, unless they have been prescribed for medical reasons.

Nowadays, as far as illicit use is concerned, barbiturates have been superseded by newer drugs and they are now a negligible aspect of the illicit drug scene in the UK. Drugs, like anything else in life, are subject to fashions and trends.

Q What are amphetamines?

Amphetamines, or speed, are chemically produced stimulants. Their action is quite different to that of barbiturates, which depress the central nervous system in a way similar to alcohol. Like barbiturates, however, they are Class C drugs and their possession is illegal unless prescribed by a doctor. Because of the risk of dependence they are seldom used nowadays for medical purposes.

Amphetamines were first used on a large scale during World War 2 and the Vietnam War to improve the performance of troops. In the 1950s and 1960s they were used to treat depression and as appetite suppressants, much like barbiturates, despite their completely different type of action.

They were used illegally on quite a wide scale during the teenage 'mod' years of the 1960s, when they were freely available in pill form. There are now signs of an increase in their popularity. They are now available as illicitly produced amphetamine sulphate powder and are the second most popular drug after cannabis.

Q **Cocaine seems to be the 'big' illicit drug at the moment. How and when did it come to prominence?**

Cocaine is derived from the leaves of the Andean coca plant, so is a naturally occurring substance. It acts principally as a stimulant, like amphetamines.

Native South Americans have probably been chewing coca leaves to get a high for thousands of years and, in some parts of South America, they still chew the leaf to gain energy and stamina.

Cocaine was first extracted from the coca plant in

1855, after which it became a popular stimulant and tonic. Until 1904, the drink Coca-Cola contained small quantities of cocaine but the recipe has since been changed.

In the UK, during World War 1, there were reports of prostitutes in London supplying cocaine to soldiers who had come home on leave. Subsequent reports and rumours – mainly unfounded – of people going crazy under the influence of cocaine led to its prohibition under the Dangerous Drugs Act of 1920.

Since then it has been illegal and has gained a reputation as the rich person's drug because of its cost. It is known in some circles as 'the champagne drug'. It is a controlled drug, classified as a Class A dangerous substance. It is still occasionally used for topical anaesthesia in dentistry and some other legitimate medical purposes.

Q What is the difference between cocaine and crack?

Crack, or crack cocaine, is a derivative of cocaine produced by separating the cocaine 'base' from its hydrochloric salt. All that is required is some genuine cocaine, water, baking soda and a microwave oven. Crack melts and vapourizes and acts more quickly than cocaine, giving an intense and immediate sense of well-being, exhilaration, physical strength and mental capacity.

Crack itself is not a new drug, but represents a new method of taking cocaine. It is taken as a powder and first made inroads into the Afro-Caribbean drug scene, from where it has spread out to the wider youth culture. It is associated with Jamaican 'yardies'.

Q Are tranquillizers taken illegally as drugs?

Tranquillizers, or benzodazepines, are depressants. They came into prominence in the 1960s as replacements for barbiturates, because of their effectiveness and apparent lack of adverse side effects. They are available only on prescription and it is illegal to supply them other than for *bona fide* medical reasons; they are not manufactured illicitly.

However, prescribed or stolen tranquillizers are available on the illicit market and are used either to tide people over times when their main drug is unavailable, to enhance the effects of other depressant or sedative-type drugs, e.g. alcohol or opiates, or to offset the effects of stimulants, e.g. ecstasy and amphetamines. In some circles, injectable temazepam has become the chosen substitute for heroin and is also sometimes used to 'come down' from the effects of stimulants.

Q What about other drugs?

The nitrites, amyl nitrite and butyl nitrite (or poppers) are quite extensively used to enhance sexual pleasure and are very much part of the gay scene. They act as a muscle relaxant, thus making anal intercourse easier.

Amyl nitrite was discovered in 1856 and first used to treat heart conditions. In the USA, amyl nitrite is classified as a Prescription Only drug, but butyl nitrite, chemically similar but with no known medical uses, is more commonly available these days. It is commonly sold in sex shops in bottles and there are no legal restrictions on its availability.

Solvents are not illegal either. When their vapours are inhaled, these carbon-based compounds produce anaesthetic-like effects. It is an offence in some areas to sell solvents in the knowledge that they are going to be used as drugs but enforcing this law is virtually impossible.

Anabolic steroids are a group of hormones which occur naturally in the body and are responsible for the development of the reproductive organs and male characteristics. They are Prescription Only drugs but, although they are not controlled or illegal, their non-medical use is increasing. They are distributed mainly through gyms, body-building clubs, etc. They are often used to make people feel more aggressive and 'masculine', and to enhance athletic performance.

Q Do drugs enhance perception, as has been claimed?

Those drugs which actually enhance perception are the hallucinogens, such as LSD and cannabis. But all drugs are used to alter – if not enhance – the mind in some way or another. Whether the apparently altered perceptions are beneficial is debatable.

All psychotropic drugs and substances, legal or illegal, are used for one purpose only: to make people feel better. If drugs made people feel worse without any enhancing effects, nobody would take them. The problems facing those who treat drug abusers is why they feel bad in the first place, and why they feel they need to turn to a psychotropic drug for relief. Clearly, they have used the drug for a specific purpose and, as nature abhors a vacuum, what do you replace the drug with if you are going to try and live without it?

Why do these drugs remain illegal?

This is a good question – and one to which there is no satisfactory answer. Campaigns for the legalization of cannabis have been going on in many countries since the 1960s and have been mostly unsuccessful. There are also now small-scale campaigns to legalize hard drugs, such as heroin and cocaine. There are arguments both for and against the legalization of drugs.

Those against legalization of psychotropic drugs argue that:

1. There are already enough addictive substances, e.g. alcohol, tobacco and caffeine, freely available, so why make things worse?

2. The legal status of alcohol and tobacco does not wipe out problems associated with abuse.

3. Legalizing drugs would result in more addicts with all the personal misery this causes plus the extra burden on the health and other related services.

4. Dangerous and potentially lethal substances should not be made more easily available.

Those in favour of legalization offer the following main arguments:

1. In moderation, cannabis and certain other drugs are no more addictive or dangerous than alcohol or tobacco and hard drugs are far less dangerous than many people believe.

2. Making drugs illegal has not stopped dedicated people from using them but has, inevitably, brought them into contact with criminals.

3. Most of the dangers connected with drugs stem from adulterated supplies rather than the drugs themselves and, if purity could be guaranteed, and prices lowered, the criminal element would be removed.

4. Legalization will not create addicts any more than legally obtainable alcohol creates alcoholics. Prohibition in the USA did not create a nation of non-drinkers – people just found their own ways of manufacturing alcohol illegally.

There are also other considerations. At the moment, governments make huge sums of money from taxing legally addictive substances, such as alcohol and tobacco, and, if drugs were to be legalized, they might lose their revenue on these items. On the other hand, it could be argued that governments could easily tax supplies in the same way that other addictive substances are taxed.

There also remains the question of how such drugs, if legalized, could be made available. Would they be sold in ordinary shops, in chemists or drug stores, on prescription? Would they come with warning labels? This is a very difficult issue with strong arguments on both sides and will not be easily resolved. The fact remains that no one actually knows what the effects of wholesale legalization would be.

Q We are told that some drugs are not addictive, while others are. What is the difference?

It depends what you mean by addiction. There are two types, physical and psychological, and they are inter-related.

Physical dependence is brought on by a bio-chemical reaction in which the drug replaces the body's natural opiates. These drugs are very few and include heroin. The brain normally makes its own opiate-like painkillers, known as endogenous morphines or endorphins, and, when heroin is introduced into the body, the body stops making its own supply of painkillers and becomes dependent on the outside source. The cravings which result always occur when body cells have come to depend on a regular supply of a substance for their workings. This also happens with tobacco and alcohol, both extremely addictive substances.

Psychological addiction varies in degree according to the drug. Although the body itself does not come to rely on the substance, the feelings experienced when using the drug are so intense, so pleasurable, or so soothing, that there is a strong desire to experience them again. This can happen not just with drugs, both legal and illegal, but also with sex, alcohol, gambling and certain foods.

The personality of the user also seems to play a part in addiction. Some researchers believe that certain people have addictive personalities, in that they easily become addicted to mind-altering substances or activities. This is attributed to people being dissatisfied or ill at ease with their normal selves. At first, taking the drug makes them feel more normal, or more like the selves they would prefer to be, e.g. more outgoing, more calm, less repressed and inhibited. The danger with psychotropic drugs is that, although they induce intensely pleasurable feelings at first, in time the user comes to crave them just to take away the pain of not having them. Dependence arises when the body, state of mind, or both, simply seems unable to do without the drug.

With highly addictive drugs, tolerance increases so that increasingly greater doses of the substance are needed to gain the same effect. This is certainly the case with heroin. Users may only realize that they are addicted when they try to do without the substance.

Q Do drug addicts often use more than one type of drug?

Eventually, yes. The majority of addicts are multiple drug users and usually also drink alcohol and smoke cigarettes. Indeed susceptible or vulnerable people rarely use just one type of mind-altering drug.

Q If these drugs are illegal, where do people get them from?

A variety of sources. They may be illegally imported, stolen, manufactured, or obtained from legal sources and then diverted. For those intent on obtaining drugs, access does not seem to be a problem, although the fact that drugs are illegal tends to make them very expensive.

Q Are they easily accessible?

Yes, in spite of police crackdowns and clampdowns. Drugs such as cannabis are easily obtainable in all large cities, and cocaine, crack and ecstasy are on sale at most raves. Anyone who wants to take these drugs seems to have no difficulty in obtaining them, although there may be problems in paying for them as dependence develops.

Q How much do they cost?

Costs vary. In 1995, in the UK, approximate prices were as follows: a bottle of butyl nitrite £5; illicitly obtained benzodiazepines £1 for four 5mg tablets; illicit amphetamine £10–£15 per gram of white powder; 50 per cent pure cocaine £80–£100 a gram and crack £25 a gram; heroin £100 a gram (addicts might use 0.25g each day); cannabis £70 per 28g (1oz) for the herbal variety and £15 per 7g (¼ oz) for the resin (five joints a day would use up this amount in a week); LSD £5 a tablet (three or four would be needed for a full-blown hallucinogenic experience); ecstasy £25 a tablet; anabolic steroids £20 for 100 tablets.

Q How are these drugs mainly taken?

Smoked, snorted, swallowed or injected. Most non-addicts feel particular horror at injecting, mainly because they can imagine swallowing or sniffing, but cannot easily see themselves injecting. With many drugs, however, this is the quickest way of gaining the effect.

For addicts, the natural human reluctance to inject is overcome because the sensations are so instantly pleasant. Injecting, usually known as 'main-lining', is more dangerous than other methods of delivery for several reasons:

(a) Veins are not designed for this continuous onslaught and abuse.

(b) Purity of supplies cannot be guaranteed.

(c) Needles are not always sterile, clean and new.

(d) Once injection has become the only route to Nirvana, the need has become desperate indeed.

Dedicated cocaine users may inject 15 times a day.

Q Are men more likely than women to take drugs?

Yes, it seems so. There are about three male addicts for every female. Whether this is because men are more adventurous or are more likely to internalize mental distress than women is not yet known. Most women who take heroin are, it seems, introduced to it by a boyfriend.

It is interesting to note that more men than women attempt or commit suicide. It also seems that, in the case of cannabis, most women only smoke a joint which has been rolled for them by a man – at least initially, even if they go on to become dedicated users. This suggests that women may have a stronger sense of self-preservation than men and may prove a fruitful line of research.

There are signs that, when women are subjected to the same stresses and strains as men, e.g. in the City, they are just as likely to take cocaine but, for the moment, drug taking is an overwhelmingly male preserve. Women who are desperate, or are suffering from severe mental and emotional distress, seem more likely to succumb to eating disorders than to take drugs. Anorexia, bulimia and compulsive eating are overwhelmingly female manifestations of a similar internal turmoil.

At the same time, women are overwhelmingly the major consumers of prescription tranquillizers. It is possible that women tend to avoid illegal drugs because they are reluctant to come into contact with the criminal fraternity. Despite this, more women than ever before *are* taking illegal drugs so maybe, one day, their numbers will equal those of men.

Q Who is most likely to take illegal drugs?

These days, anyone at all, from members of the affluent classes to unemployed teenagers from rough housing estates. As drugs are illegal, accurate figures are hard to come by, but there seems little doubt that use is on the increase all the time. In the 1960s, it seemed very daring to use cannabis, but now there is hardly a person under 25 years old in the UK who has not used it, at least occasionally.

When it comes to hard drugs, figures are even more unreliable. A 1993 survey by market research firm Mintel showed that, in the UK, there had been a marked increase in drug use by young people and, between 1989 and 1992, the numbers of 15- to 24-year olds using both hard and soft drugs had doubled from 16 to 29 per cent of all people in this age group. Hard drug use tripled from 2 to 7 per cent.

We know that illicit drug use is increasing all the time, but because drugs are illegal and statistics are unreliable, accurate figures are hard to obtain. In 1993, in the UK, 27,976 heroin addicts were notified to the Home Office – an increase of 13 per cent on the previous year. 40 per cent of these were newly registered. Notifications for cocaine increased by 26 per cent in 1993 compared with the previous year.

Q Are all drug users young?

No. Although the use of illegal drugs is regarded as part of the youth scene, many middle-aged and older people are drug addicts. A Harley Street doctor, convicted recently of peddling and using illegal drugs, was in his sixties and had been an addict, apparently, for over 30 years.

Although the habit mainly starts in youth, as with drinking and smoking, it may persist into middle and even old age. Old people sometimes turn to heroin to combat pain, loneliness and depression. Elderly people are more likely to become dependent on drugs because of metabolic changes associated with ageing. Although most anti-drug publicity is directed at teenagers and young people, recreational drug use is by no means confined to the under-30s.

2 The Effects of Drugs

Q How would you describe the effects of mind-altering drugs?

There are now a great number of drugs on the market, all varying considerably in their effects, so each must be discussed individually. Generally speaking, however, all drugs deliver feelings and sensations which are difficult, if not impossible, to obtain in any other way.

It is easy for those who have never tried, or never been tempted to try, psychotropic drugs to condemn both the drugs and the users. Those who have experienced their effects know just how seductive they can be, and how alluring the sensations that they deliver. But, as with all experiences in life, there is a price to pay and, often, the greater the sensation, the higher the price in terms of money, health, addictive potential and dependence.

In its 1994 Drug Abuse Briefing, the Institute for the Study of Drug Dependence points out that the vast majority of people who use drugs come to no harm and many feel that they have greatly benefited from the improved social, intellectual or physical performance that some drugs can deliver. They might, for example, feel more relaxed and better able to communicate in a social situation. Nevertheless, the Drug Abuse Briefing also shows that psychotropic drugs are capable of impairing performance, perception and the ability to carry out tasks such as driving, operating machinery; they may also over-ride the need for sleep or food.

The degree of danger and risk, however, depends on how the drugs are taken, for what reason, and how often. Health can be seriously damaged by smoking 80 cigarettes or drinking 20 cups of tea or coffee a day. But, just as most people do not drink coffee or smoke this amount, so most people do not use drugs in such an abandoned, uncontrolled way.

Cannabis can be a disappointing experience when taken for the first time because, often, nothing very much seems to happen. New users have to learn which effects to look out for and these generally consist of, a pleasurable state of relaxation and an enhanced sense of colour, light and sound. This may be accompanied by a feeling of anxiety. Higher doses can bring about a distortion in time – time seems to pass much more slowly – and distress and confusion may also occur. These effects usually start a few minutes after smoking a joint and can last for several hours. Once the effect wears off, there may be a sense of weariness or heaviness.

LSD is a powerful hallucinogen and many myths have grown up around its use, mainly because the drug has been associated with hippies, unconventional people and 'beat' writers. Nowadays, it has taken its place among the pantheon of drugs and is not considered special in any way. A 'trip' starts about an hour after taking the drug and experiences differ widely while the trip lasts. Some people have a full-blown psychedelic experience, while others just notice intensified colours, shapes and sounds. True hallucinations are quite rare, although perceptions will usually be distorted. The emotional effects of LSD can include heightened self-awareness and a sense of having mystical or spiritual experiences. Practised users say that LSD can be taken to guide them towards the kind of trip they wish to have.

Heroin, probably still seen as the most dangerous drug in the popular imagination, has a powerful sedative effect. It has the power to lock out emotional pain and users will experience a rush of pleasure as the drug takes effect. There is a kind of 'click', say users, as suffering vanishes under its powerful influence. The feeling of relaxation and freedom from pain, of being cocooned in warmth and safety, is, as one user described it, 'exquisitely sweet.' Once this feeling has been experienced, users will endure almost anything – even injecting – to regain it.

Cocaine has a quite different effect. Instead of depressing everything, it heightens all sensations and delivers a feeling of exhilaration, well-being, lack of hunger, indifference to pain and increased energy levels. Usually sniffed up the nose, it delivers its effects within about 30 minutes of being taken. When smoked as crack the effects are more immediate but, at the same time, more short-lived. If large doses are taken, this feeling of heightened well-being can be replaced by panic or anxiety attacks, paranoia and, in some cases, hallucination. After-effects of cocaine use may include tiredness and depression.

Amphetamines act on the body in much the same way as adrenaline, intensifying everything. Heart rate increases, pupils dilate and appetite decreases. There is an instant feeling of increased alertness, confidence and cheerfulness. With larger doses, a manic state can result, with a rapid flow of ideas and a sensation of great mental and physical capacity. The downside can be greater anxiety and restlessness and even, if high doses are repeated over several days, sensations of delirium, panic and hallucination. 'Amphetamine psychosis', a feeling of being persecuted, is a well-known side effect of large doses. Effects from a single dose last 3 to 4 hours and result in fatigue, rather like the feeling one gets after huge adrenaline-fuelled exertion.

With ecstasy, a single tablet is usually taken and the profound effects occur within half an hour. These include an intense feeling of elation and euphoria, enhanced perception and aesthetic pleasure from immediate surroundings. Social anxiety and shyness are considerably reduced. This effect lasts for several hours. There are no lasting ill effects from occasional use, but there will be nausea and dehydration. Ecstasy makes the user very thirsty and there may be muscle ache, sweating, pupil dilation and blurred vision. If there is severe dehydration, death may result and, in fact, all deaths from ecstasy have occurred in this way. If the user keeps drinking water, he or she has little to worry about but, as ecstasy is taken mainly at raves, dehydration is often further increased by dancing and the warm atmosphere of a crowded room.

Barbiturates have been largely superseded by other drugs but have been valued for their guaranteed calming effect. A small dose makes users feel relaxed, sociable and good-humoured.

The short-term immediate effects of all the drugs mentioned so far are to make people feel less shy, less inhibited and less anxious, in short, how they would like to feel all the time, but cannot without the aid of a drug. The effect from small doses is exactly the same as that from one or two alcoholic drinks – pleasurable intoxication – but, as with alcohol, coordination, speech, increased emotion and tearfulness are common side effects. When injected, barbiturates produce instant feelings of warmth, pleasure and safety, much like injected heroin.

Amyl and butyl nitrite take effect instantly once inhaled and produce feelings of lightheadedness within minutes. Usually taken to enhance sexual pleasure, users report better orgasms and prevention of premature ejaculation. Butyl nitrite is the main ingredient of 'delay sprays', although these probably have little, if any, effect. Used mainly by men within the gay community, nitrites also produce headaches, dizziness, a flushed face and increased heart rate. There may also be nausea, cold sweats and feelings of weakness. Nitrites should not be used by anyone with a history of heart trouble.

Benzodiazepines, or tranquillizers, act rather like barbiturates and depress the function of all body systems. At the same time, they relieve tension and anxiety and make users feel calm and relaxed. Most users report a lightening of anxiety and panic rather than positive feelings of pleasure and, for this reason, as well as the fact that they can be legally obtained on doctor's prescription, they are not particularly popular as recreational drugs.

Q These are all the immediate effects. What about the long-term effects?

Again, these differ according to the drug. Much depends on the method of delivery, how much of the drug has been taken, and for how long. Also, as with any substance, the effects vary from user to user.

Long-term effects from cannabis do not seem to differ markedly from the short-term effects and, so far, there are no studies which show severe adverse reactions, even when cannabis has been taken regularly for many years.

If cannabis is smoked, there may be a greater risk of bronchitis, and possibly lung cancer, as with cigarette smoking, but studies have not confirmed this. Cannabis does not produce physical dependence so there should be no problems from withdrawal although, as with drinking alcohol, users may, over the years, come to rely on cannabis to help them through social situations. Despite the occasional scare story, serious complications are extremely rare and hardly merit a mention.

With hard drugs of course, the situation is different. Although serious long-term ill-effects may be rare, they are a definite possibility. In the case of heroin, tolerance develops quickly, so that increasingly larger doses of the drug become necessary to gain the same effect. In time, therefore, it is taken not to enhance pleasure or relaxation, but just to feel normal. The physiological effects of long-term opiate use do not, in themselves, seem to be serious but withdrawal symptoms may include respiratory conditions and constipation – a chronic problem with heroin users. The main dangers are related to the principal method of delivery, i.e. injection, but these arise from the lifestyle of the users, and the possible adulteration of supplies, rather than the actual heroin itself. Adulterants can cause breathing problems, skin disorders, tetanus and decreased appetite, and dirty needles can spread infection.

LSD also has a fearsome reputation but there are no known dangers from long-term or repeated use. Psychotic episodes, bad trips and frightening hallucinations, may all occur, but there is no evidence that chronic brain damage or mental illness is inevitable, although a few users have become mentally ill. Because there is no physical dependence on the drug, the effects are not dose-related, and even psychological dependence on the drug is relatively rare.

Ecstasy has acquired a sleazy kind of glamour and has been associated with deaths. The main side effect of this drug is intense dehydration, which can result in death in rare cases. There is also some indication of an association between pro-longed use and liver damage, but this is as yet unconfirmed. There is no physical dependence and no bad withdrawal symptoms. There is also, as yet, no evidence of it being used for more than a year or two. The majority of users are occasional, enjoying the trip and the high, but using it only once in a while. Some studies have indicated that ecstasy can cause lasting brain damage and at least one important brain chemical has been reported as being reduced or defective in long-term users. One study, carried out by researchers Dr Una McCann and Dr George Ricaurte of John Hopkins University, Baltimore, showed that, compared with controls, ecstasy users had lower levels of a brain chemical associated with mood changes. However, the sample – 30 users and 28 controls - was very small, so the results are not conclusive.

Cocaine does not create physical dependence, nor are there bad withdrawal problems from its long-term use. However, a strong psychological dependence often develops because of the benefits it appears to deliver. The sensations of physical and mental well-being are not easily achieved by any other route. With repeated use, however, these feelings are replaced by restlessness, excitability, nausea, insomnia and weight loss. When this happens, users may discontinue the drug of their own accord, with no lengthy detoxification or rehabilitation being necessary. The main damage from long-term cocaine snorting is to the membranes and tissues in the nose. There are special dangers, of course, from injecting, but these are the same risks that frequent injection of any drug always carry. The dangers from crack are exactly the same as those from ordinary cocaine.

Long-term use of amphetamines can cause psychological dependence because users may feel lethargic, hungry and deeply depressed when they are no longer taking the drug. As with all stimulants, amphetamines do not replace hunger, tiredness and lack of energy but merely put off the evil hour – the body always catches up and its demands cannot be over-ridden for ever. As tolerance develops, users may be tempted to take increasingly larger doses until, eventually toxic symptoms develop; these may include delusions, hallucinations, paranoia and hostility to others. One of the principle long-term dangers from any artificial stimulant are the depletion of the body's natural resistance to disease. Because amphetamines raise blood pressure, prolonged use may also cause heart failure via damage to blood vessels.

Solvents are used mainly by secondary-school children in socially deprived areas and long-term use is virtually unknown. For most children, glue sniffing is a short-term stage which they go through, although it may lead to a drug habit. Very long-term use of solvents can cause damage to the brains and kidneys and, if leaded petrol is sniffed, lead poisoning. However, these cases of serious damage from long-term use remain relatively isolated. Tolerance to solvents can develop and there may be withdrawal symptoms, but there seems to be no actual physical dependence. As with most drugs, long-term problems appear only when the user has serious personality, behavioural or family problems –

usually a mixture of all three – which led him or her to start relying on solvents as an escape in the first place.

The dangers from long-term benzodiazepine (tranquillizer) use have been well documented in cases of people using the drugs legally, and problems with illegal users are the same. There can be intense withdrawal problems, because of physical dependence on the drug itself and because whatever problems led the user to rely on the drug in the first place will once again come to the forefront, usually magnified.

All sedatives, all psychotropic drugs, just conceal underlying problems; they never send them away. One tranquillizer user, who had given up after 25 years of use, said that the first thing she thought of was her divorce – her reason for taking the drugs in the first place. Although tranquillizers had helped her over a difficult patch, the eventual result was to create two problems where there had been only one before.

 How do drugs affect sexual performance?

Men who are addicted to heroin are almost always impotent, because heroin damps down all body systems, including the capacity for erection.

Cocaine initially heightens arousal in men and women, because of the euphoria associated with its use, but habitual users will experience the opposite sensations – depression, low self-esteem, fatigue and anxiety. There may also be hallucinations and paranoia if use continues and both men and women will become incapable of orgasm.

Cannabis, being essentially a relaxant, can eventually lead to lack of interest in sex and also has the effect of drying out natural secretions and lubrication.

Amphetamines can lead to impotence in male users and an inability to ejaculate. Female users eventually lose the capacity for orgasm.

Butyl nitrite (poppers) is used almost exclusively as an aphrodisiac. However, there is no way of permanently improving sexual performance through use of drugs and, eventually, all drugs, illegal and prescribed, will lead to a diminution of sexual interest and performance. Any substance sold for this purpose is either useless or dangerous.

Q Are there more dangers for women than men in drug taking?

The main additional dangers for women come from factors to do with sex and reproduction: conception, fertility, pregnancy and childbirth.

Although there has been very little reliable research in this area, because many of the drugs are illegal and there are difficulties in carrying out proper research, certain facts have become known. One is that, in all users under the influence of all psychotropic drugs, including alcohol, resistance to sex may be lowered and women risk having unprotected sex with partners who they might not choose in other circumstances. Proper contraceptive measures may not be taken and unplanned pregnancies may result. This risk is clearly not shared by male drug users, although their sexual behaviour and attitudes may also be affected by drug taking.

Some drugs, e.g. heroin, can interfere with the menstrual cycle, which, in turn, may make effective contraception difficult. But although heroin interferes with periods, it does not necessarily make women infertile. Amphetamines may cause menstruation to cease and may prevent ovulation.

Women drug users who become pregnant, either accidentally or on purpose, often wonder whether it is safe to stop using their drug. As far as amphetamines, ecstasy, cannabis, LSD and cocaine are concerned, the answer is yes, because physical dependence does not develop. With opiate-derived drugs, e.g. heroin and its synthetic substitute, methadone, medical opinion is divided. Obviously, it is better not to be using drugs such as heroin when pregnant but sudden withdrawal may be dangerous; prescribed doses from a doctor may be the best option.

It is not beneficial to stop taking tranquillizers or barbiturates suddenly – or any other drugs with a physical dependence – and, again, medical help should be sought at the earliest opportunity.

The Institute for the Study of Drug Dependence believes that there is a moral objection to women using drugs and point out that the vast majority of women who do use hard drugs also smoke, drink, are probably unemployed, have bad housing and are poorly nourished, all of which can harm the foetus and the developing child.

This demonstrates the difficulty in separating the dangers of the drug itself from the social factors that frequently lead to a drug habit developing.

The risks to a baby from an established habit include: low birthweight, withdrawal symptoms from the drug, and increased risk of cot death. A cocaine habit may cause the placenta to separate from the foetus and therefore induce miscarriage. Research is continuing into the likelihood of babies, particularly those of heavy and long-established users, being born with withdrawal symptoms from cocaine use.

Q What about HIV and AIDS?

There has been debate and controversy over the possible connections between drug use and the onset of HIV and AIDS since the early 1980s. Final conclusions have not been reached by any means and research continues today. However, two important connections have been made.

1. Drug users are at risk of contracting the HIV virus and developing AIDS if they share injecting equipment that is infected. So drug use can play a part in the transmission of HIV/AIDS from one person to another.

2. Prolonged drug use takes a heavy toll on the body and persistent use of intravenous drugs over a long period of time severely affects the body's immune system, in some cases causing

it to collapse. Poor diet can be a factor in this as heavy drug users often do not eat properly, partly because drugs like heroin and amphetamines depress the appetite and partly because users may prefer to spend their money on drugs rather than on food. This can have a serious effect on someone who is already HIV positive. It may increase their chances of developing full-blown AIDS if an immune system which is already vulnerable is subject to additional depression by heavy drug use.

3 Treatment

Q What should I do if I suspect my child is on drugs?

The most important thing is not to over-react – or even to imagine that there is much you can do, although this is more easily said than done. Parents nowadays tend to worry constantly about the possibility of their children taking drugs but, in practice, there is little they can do to stop them. The best thing you can do is to learn as much as you can about drugs, either through books or, if you suspect that your child is using drugs, by joining a self-help group, e.g. Families Anonymous, which will be able to give expert advice on how to handle the situation.

Many teenagers experiment with cannabis, but very few go on to try hard drugs. Many people in their early or mid-twenties will also experiment with ecstasy or, perhaps, cocaine but this does not mean they will go on to become drug addicts.

If there is one golden rule, it is this: do not hit the roof if you discover, or suspect, that your child has taken cannabis. One mother asked her

16-year-old son if he had ever been to a party where there were drugs. 'Mum,' he replied, while fixing her with a pitying gaze, 'Have I ever been to a party where there haven't been some kind of drugs?' Least said, soonest mended, is often the best policy here. Nevertheless a pupil caught taking drugs at school, will probably be expelled; no school can be seen to break the law.

Do not necessarily imagine, if your child is on hard drugs, that this has happened because he or she has inadvertently got in with the 'wrong' set. It seems, from all the evidence available, that those who are predisposed towards drug addiction will actively seek out peers and friends who are users. Young people may be attracted to the company of those using drugs because they enjoy their company, and this may include experimenting with drugs, but this in itself does not mean that they are predisposed towards drug misuse. A drug habit does not become established simply because young people copy drug users. There will be some deep underlying sadness, depression or problem, even if these are not apparent to the parents.

It is one of the hardest things in the world for parents to see their beloved children descend into drug addiction, but it is important not to try to pick up the pieces for them, or prevent them from reaping the consequences of their own actions; by the same token, do not condemn them but agree to work with them if they genuinely wish to come off the drug.

It has also been shown that nobody – parents, teachers, doctors or others – can prevent a person becoming a drug addict, or force, cajole or threaten them into giving up their substance. Recovery can happen only when the user fervently wishes it and no longer desires to be a drug user.

Q Is there any way a parent can prevent a drug problem?

There is no absolutely guaranteed way, although there are things parents can do to lessen the risk. Of these, the most important is to set an example of good behaviour. Children learn above all by example and are far less likely to turn to drugs if the parents are not addicts. The children of parents who are on tranquillizers, or who smoke or drink heavily are far more likely to become addicted to drugs than those of parents who do not depend on some mind-altering substance to get them through the day.

Another thing which parents can do is to make sure that they instill a positive attitude into their children, so that they grow up with a strong sense of self-worth and self-esteem. There is abundant evidence to show that addicts, particularly heroin addicts, have very little sense of self-worth or self-confidence.

Young people who grow up with an inner, unshakeable core of self-confidence are unlikely to become addicted to drugs, although they may of course experiment with them. All young people who turn to drugs, other than for purely experimental purposes, are, or perceive themselves to be, emotionally deprived and lacking in love.

Parents can prepare themselves by learning as much about drugs as possible. Children will respect parents who seem to know what they are talking about and who appreciate that drugs can induce good feelings as well as being addictive.

A Government survey on parents and drugs revealed that, while condemning drugs whole-heartedly, most parents were at the same time extremely ill-informed about their effects and whether the use of soft drugs could lead to hard drugs. Children who suspect that their parents do not know what they are talking about will take no notice of what they say about drugs. Indeed, most children are far better informed about drugs these days than their parents.

The vast majority of drug addicts come from broken or loveless homes.

How can you spot a drug user?

There are some early warning signs, which can often be missed: a noticeable alteration in attitude, consciousness or mood; and extreme manic happiness followed by black depression. Neither of these are absolutely positive signs of drug use, but they may well provide some indication.

Unusual sleepiness or drowsiness should also be noted. The classic symptom of heroin use is tiny, pin-point pupils. Other signs include: loss of appetite and interest in former hobbies, sport, school or friends; telling lies; furtive behaviour; money or valuables disappearing; and unusual smells, stains or marks on the body. Peculiar-looking powders, capsules, heated tinfoil or needles and syringes should also be regarded with extreme suspicion. Most young users are too clever to leave telltale signs about the house, but they cannot always conceal their mood.

Parents who believe they have good reason to suspect that a child is using drugs should never be angry because this could exacerbate the problem. Parental disapproval only adds to the already enormous burden the child is carrying and it is best to show that, although you do not love the drug habit, you still love the child.

The most important thing to realize is that drug addiction is an illness which needs professional understanding and care. Love and understanding alone may not be enough to help a child overcome an addiction problem.

Q How easy is it to diagnose drug taking?

It is easy enough to diagnose from a urine sample, provided that a doctor can get hold of a sample. Traces of drugs can be detected in the urine for up to 3 or 4 days after use, but addicts are so devious that it is not unknown for them to substitute urine samples from non-users.

The latest method to detect drug use is hair analysis, a technique developed in the early 1980s by Dr Werner Baumgartner, an American chemist. It is so accurate, according to its supporters, that it detected traces of opium in the 170-year-old sample of hair from the poet John Keats. Traces of drugs are deposited in the hair and remain there. Analysts can tell, using a month's growth of hair, exactly which drugs have been taken during that period.

One addiction specialist, Dr Colin Brewer, uses hair analysis at the Stapleford Centre, a private drug rehabilitation centre in London. He said: 'Urine samples are relatively easy to evade, whereas hair testing is not.' After all, it is not so easy to swap samples when these are taken from your own hair by the doctor and only a tiny sample of hair is needed to make a correct analysis.

Hair analysis is being used increasingly to diagnose drug taking.

Q Which drug is most associated with serious addiction problems today?

Without a doubt, heroin. Although most drug users will eventually take anything they can get hold of, it is heroin – or at least, injection of heroin – which seems to do the most damage. Heroin is the most widely abused drug and addicts eventually suffer serious health breakdowns – although there are cases of people who have been on maintenance doses of heroin with no apparent overwhelming problems for years.

The other aspect is that heroin is a Class A controlled drug and addiction is therefore viewed very seriously.

Cocaine is not physically addictive in the same way as heroin, but it is a habit which can escalate, be very expensive and difficult to treat.

Q What are the criteria for being a drug addict?

There is no absolute definition of a drug addict, but anybody who has become hopelessly dependent on drugs and cannot live without them can be considered an addict.

Q What is the law governing heroin use by registered addicts?

Since 1969, only a very few doctors have been allowed to prescribe heroin to registered addicts; others can prescribe the synthetic substitute, opiate methadone. The original idea behind the prescription of the drug itself, or its substitute, was that, by making it available through official channels, illegal suppliers would be driven out and supplies could be regulated.

While the UK set up hospital treatment centres to treat addicts by prescribing carefully controlled doses of their substance, the rest of the Western world looked on in amazement. In 1974 an American writer, Horace Freelance Judson, wrote in *Heroin Addiction in Britain*: 'What everybody knows about the British and heroin is that they supply it on prescription to addicts'. The situation today is that nobody can agree on exactly how to treat heroin addiction.

Some people working with drug addicts believe that the amounts of heroin or methadone prescribed to registered addicts is too low, therefore encouraging them to make up the difference with street supplies and to continue in the lifestyle which prescription of the drug was intended to prevent.

Q Are doctors reluctant to prescribe maintenance heroin?

On the whole, yes. Doctors very rarely prescribe maintenance heroin for two reasons.

(a) Addicts may sell their scrips to pay for cheaper, street drugs, thus making doctors involuntary illegal suppliers.

(b) Many doctors assume that tolerance is infinite, and that use will spiral ever upwards.

This leads those doctors who are allowed to prescribe heroin to do so in doses which, according to some experts, are ineffective.

There is an arbitrary maximum dose of intravenous heroin, adopted by the majority of doctors who prescribe it, of 100 mg a day. One worker in drug dependence, Allan Parry, writing in *The Lancet* in February 1992, believes that maintenance doses of 300-400 mg a day are more realistic. This dosage means that heroin addicts become less inclined to resort to street drugs and can maintain a steady, genial state with no great harm to themselves or others.

Q What are the main methods of treatment given by doctors?

There are four principal prescribing options. The choice will partly depend on the doctor and partly on the patient. Ideally, a treatment programme should be worked out in discussion with the patient and the doctor. If you go to your doctor with a heroin problem, you will usually be offered one of the following treatment options.

(a) Rapid withdrawal aims to detoxify the user as quickly as possible, using oral methadone in decreasing doses over a number of weeks. This is ideal for users who have already arranged to be admitted to a rehabilitation house and who must be drug-free before admission.

(b) Gradual withdrawal follows a similar pattern but extends over months rather than weeks. This option is suitable for pregnant users who wish to withdraw from the drug before having a baby.

(c) Maintenance to abstinence is suitable for those patients who require maintenance, usually on methadone, while other aspects of their lives are being stabilized. Although the ultimate aim is abstinence, there may be severe social, physical or psychological problems to deal with before the drug addiction is tackled. In these cases, doctors will usually liaise with specialist clinics, especially if the patient finds any reduction in dose difficult to deal with.

(d) Maintenance is for those users who are not aiming for immediate abstinence, and so prescribing may be for an indefinite time.

In some cases, injectable opiates may be prescribed.

Q What makes users seek treatment?

Sometimes users may be referred to a treatment centre after contracting another illness, being admitted in hospital, or being found guilty of committing a criminal act. Just occasionally, they seek treatment of their own accord but, as with all addictions, this happens usually only when they have reached their personal rock bottom.

It has been proved time and again that nobody can persuade a drug addict to seek help. Unless an addict sincerely wants to kick the habit, he or she will resist every attempt at treatment.

Q How does instant withdrawal work?

At City Roads, an old-established, short-term residential drug rehabilitation centre in north London, UK, the aim is to help users return to a satisfying and useful drug-free life. The Centre has teams of nurses, social workers, health visitors and doctors on hand, and users can either self-refer or be referred by friends, relatives or doctors.

Cases seen at this clinic are mainly the desperate ones. Users who are referred to crisis centres such as City Roads are not, on the whole, just using cannabis; they may be using cocaine, heroin, barbiturates, amphetamines or, more usually, a mixture of anything they can get.

At City Roads the aim is to get the addict off the drug instantly. The physical symptoms of withdrawal, however traumatic they may be at the time, disappear after a few days but breaking the emotional dependence can be very hard.

City Roads likes to take in people for about 3 weeks, so that they can have experienced counselling and help in leading a drug-free life in future. There is the understanding that detoxification is only one step towards keeping people off drugs in the long term, and people often return more than once to go through the programme.

The success rate of City Roads is 30 per cent drug free after a year. This does not sound very high, but gives an indication of how difficult it can be for a person to remain drug free once a habit has become established.

Q How do street (community) agencies work?

The aim of these agencies is to seek out drug users who are not already having treatment. Most of their clients are young – under 25-years-old – and are not registered with, or under, a doctor's care. Most will be pursuing a chaotic lifestyle and may well be homeless. There are about 40 of these agencies in the UK and they offer advice by personal contact or telephone. Both users and their families can contact the agency for specific advice and counselling on how to cope with a drug problem.

These agencies also provide a referral service for those who may need hospital treatment or long-term residential care. Young users may find it easier to contact one of these friendly, approachable agencies than the family doctor. Workers at these centres are all very experienced and know how to handle difficult clients, especially those who have mixed feelings about coming off their drugs, i.e. a high proportion of users.

Q How do hospital clinics work?

There are, at the time of writing, about 100 National Health Service hospitals, throughout the

UK, which offer detoxification and rehabilitation, but referral from a doctor is essential.

Hospital facilities vary. Some have full-time clinics staffed by well-motivated teams of doctors, social workers, psychologists and nurses; some have clinics which are open for only a few hours a week; others have residential withdrawal facilities. Treatment methods also vary and range from maintenance to instant withdrawal.

Unfortunately hospitals do not, on the whole, have a very good record for getting addicts off their drugs permanently. They also all have long waiting lists and very limited catchment areas.

Q Aren't there very expensive treatment centres which cost about £2,500 a week?

Yes, there are a number of these and, although very expensive, they have the best record for helping people to adopt a permanent drug-free lifestyle.

Broadway Lodge in Weston-super-Mare, UK, one of the best known of these treatment centres, has been called the 'Eton of rehabilitation houses'. This centre believes that addicts experience an aching void on withdrawal which is similar to losing a loved one, and that this has to be addressed if a drug-free lifestyle is to become permanent. Over the years, a drug becomes an intimate friend of the user and there is a long-lasting sense of bereavement when it is removed. The difference between losing a loved one and losing heroin, however, is that the drug can always come back into one's life. The underlying philosophy at Broadway is that drug addiction is a disease and that addicts may actually have a different biochemical make-up from non-addicts. The Lodge believes that the user must be helped to become responsible for his or her own actions. A very high 70 per cent success rate is claimed for its 6-week in-house programme.

Most rehabilitation houses follow the Twelve Step Minnesota Model which has proved the most consistently successful method of dealing with all addictions. These houses also take in alcoholics and treatment for alcohol and drug addiction is identical. Most drug addicts also drink alcohol, and often they will be multi-addicted. The aim, as with alcohol treatment, is sobriety for ever.

Q Do out-patient clinics work as well as in-patient centres?

Because in-patient clinics are so very expensive,

there is now a move towards out-patient day care for addicts. There are several reasons for this trend. Many addicts are full of self-pity and need a lot of help to become effective in the outside world. It seems that, in some cases, at least, there is a better chance of long-term recovery if the addict can continue to work and live at home while attending day therapy. It is also often easier to involve the family if the addict is attending a day centre near his or her home. In addition, treatment is less costly and insurance companies are more prepared to pay for it.

Q Are there any special facilities for solvent users?

No. Most drug detoxification and rehabilitation programmes have concentrated on the problems connected with heroin, or multiple drug use. Nowadays, every health authority in the UK has a Community Drugs Team and many volunteer groups but there are at present only two agencies dealing exclusively with solvent use.

Statistics show that more than 120 people a year die from inhaling lighter fuel, aerosols, glue and other solvents, compared with about 70 people a year dying from heroin abuse.

According to Richard Ives, author of three books on solvent abuse, there is a certain cachet to illegal drug use and substantial numbers of people in the 'in-crowd' have taken illegal substances. This is not the case with solvents. No beautiful people, it is perceived, take solvents and there is no author, such as Will Self, to glorify and expound on the solvent culture, as there has been with the cultures surrounding heroin, LSD and cocaine. This, he suggests, is one of the reasons for the comparative lack of interest in solvents.

On the whole, solvent users themselves are seldom attractive, articulate or appealing in any way, unlike many illegal drug users. Solvent users are typically young socially disadvantaged teenagers, almost always boys. Also, the effects of the substances are frequently short-lived. Volatile substances have fewer side effects or medical consequences than illegal substances and are almost wholly ignored by drug agencies.

There is now a national solvent abuse charity, Re-Solv, which can be contacted through the National Children's Bureau and which is looking at solvent abuse in terms of accident prevention and consumer safety. Richard Ives believes that skilled youth counsellors and schools programmes are needed to prevent the growth of solvent abuse but, at the moment, there is no real policy and, compared with the attention given to heroin, cocaine and ecstasy, no real interest.

4 Recovery

Q **Are drug addicts difficult people to help?**

Yes, very – and this is one of the problems.
People become drug addicts because they are in
some kind of deep emotional or mental pain.
They take psychotropic drugs to numb or overcome the pain but, of course, this always returns
when the effect of the drug wears off. By the time
they come for treatment, addicts have accumulated
a large number of problems.

There is the addiction itself, and the very strong
possibility that the addict's life has become so
focused on drugs that the only important thing is
the next 'fix'.

Addiction also creates denial; few people like to
admit that they are addicts, or that they are
controlled by a narcotic substance, and so their
natural inclination is to underestimate their habit.
This can make it difficult for treatment agencies to
gauge the extent of the problem.

In addition, the drug itself often causes negative
personality changes and can make people para-
noid, psychotic, suspicious and mentally ill.

Q Is withdrawal in hospital always necessary?

Not always. It depends on the severity of the addiction and on what other problems may be associated with drug use, e.g. malnutrition, infection, mental problems and physical ill health. Most doctors treating drug addicts say that the main problem is not physical withdrawal but helping the addicts to find another way of living – and this takes time, money and effort.

It must be remembered that all chronic drug addicts have established a lifestyle which revolves almost wholly around drugs. The drug has solved every problem; it has become the user's best friend; all contacts and social life revolve around it; it has taken the place of intimate relationships. The main problem for drug addicts is not so much withdrawal as rehabilitation.

Q Is it possible to withdraw from drugs at home, by yourself?

It is possible, with good care and advice, but it is far better for any one determined to withdraw to seek medical help right away. But as drug services are oversubscribed and there may be long waiting lists, some people may feel they cannot wait – otherwise the moment will pass.

This is the story of how one parent managed to help her 19-year-old son off his heroin habit, which was costing him about £150 a week. As he had no job – few addicts can manage to hold down jobs at the same time as their habit – he was having to resort to shoplifting and stealing to pay for the drugs. The family were middle-class and lived in a luxurious home on Merseyside. This is how the boy's mother describes what happened.

First of all, I asked for help from the local drug units and social services, but they were either too busy, or couldn't offer help soon enough. As my son had just been arrested for shoplifting, I felt it could go on no longer.

The only answer was to try to get my son off heroin myself. He pleaded for one last fix. I looked at this blank, staring skeleton, completely devoid of all feelings, who was still my son and I could not stop crying.

By midnight he was rolling around the floor clutching his stomach, clawing at the cramp. Then came the diarrhoea, the vomiting. By 3 am he was in unbearable agony, screaming all the time: 'help me, Mum.' We ran constant hot baths hoping that might alleviate the pain. For 60 hours it went on. Hell without break. The screams, the dreadful retching, limbs flailing, body twisted, face contorted in utter anguish.

I never left his side. We took it in turns to talk to him non-stop, hoping maybe we were getting through and letting him know we were there, that we cared.

It seemed like 60 years but the crisis was over. But for the next 12 weeks it was touch and go. Someone was with him every second of the day and night.

This is the reality of detoxification for somebody with a heavily established habit. But this mother's do-it-yourself detoxification programme worked. The court decided to put her son on probation for the shoplifting and he managed to get a job. He subsequently led a heroin-free life and settled down into a good job.

Q What is the Minnesota Model?

This is a form of treatment for drug addicts and alcoholics which was developed in the USA and has now spread all over the world. In some circles it is still regarded as controversial, because of its belief that drug addiction is, above all, a spiritual disease and that it is only by realizing this and asking for help from a 'higher power' that permanent sobriety can be achieved.

This method makes use of the 'tough love' principle, i.e. addicts must not be protected from the consequences of their behaviour. At these clinics, residents are discharged immediately if caught using drugs, regardless of whether or not they can get home. It is recognized that it is often only when addicts are confronted with the consequences of their actions that they can begin to be responsible people.

The other main aspect of the Minnesota Model is that it follows the Alcoholics Anonymous Twelve Steps in the belief that they constitute the best means of recovery. The steps are:

Step One We admitted we were powerless over drugs – that our lives had become unmanageable.

Step Two Came to believe that a Power greater than ourselves could restore us to sanity.

Step Three   Made a decision to turnout will and give our lives over to the care of God as we understood Him.

Step Four   Made a searching and fearless moral inventory of ourselves.

Step Five   Admitted to God, to ourselves and to another human being the exact nature of our wrongs.

Step Six   Were entirely ready to have God remove all these defects of character.

Step Seven   Humbly asked Him to remove our shortcomings.

Step Eight   Made a list of all persons we had harmed, and became willing to make amends to them all.

Step Nine   Made direct amends to such people wherever possible, except when to do so would injure them or others.

Step Ten   Continued to take personal inventory and when we were wrong promptly admitted it.

Step Eleven   Sought through prayer and meditation to improve our conscious contact with God *as we* understood Him, praying only for knowledge of his will for us and the power to carry that out.

Step Twelve   Having had a spiritual awakening as the result of these steps, we tried to carry this message to others, and to practice these principles in all our affairs.

Q   Do some people object to the religious overtones of these steps?

Yes, very many addicts object to it profoundly, but there are many ways of interpreting God in this context. Some people prefer to invoke their own higher power, if God has little, or a negative, meaning for them.

The point about the Minnesota Model and Twelve-Step programmes is that addicts are working towards recovery with others who have had the same experiences. Most, if not all, of the staff will also be addicts in recovery and will therefore understand exactly what it is like.

The power of the Twelve Steps is that they operate in direct opposition to the previous coping strategies of addicts, i.e. fear, shame, self-neglect. As time goes on, and the Steps become more fully understood, a transformation will take place.

Of course, not every addict will find this treatment approach acceptable, in which case there are other options available.

Q Do these rehabilitation houses offer detoxification programmes?

Only some. Nearly all residential rehabilitation centres require the client to have completed a full detoxification programme and spent at least 24 hours drug-free prior to admission. Clients are expected to remain drug-free throughout their stay and most centres are very strict about no drug use on their premises. There are about 2,000 beds in residential rehabilitation units in the UK but most are oversubscribed and there are long waiting lists. Moreover, because of the shortage of places, many drug users are unable to detoxify themselves in the community and so the problem continues. There is, however, no one solution to becoming 'clean' which will suit everybody.

Q What are the exceptions to this 'no drug' rule?

Phoenix House, an old-established rehabilitation centre, has a Families Project whereby it offers a 6-month programme for addicted parents and their children. It operates on what is known as the 'concept' model and is the largest agency in the UK, providing residential care, with projects in London, Bexhill, Sheffield, the Wirral and south Tyneside. Its methods were developed to meet the needs of the long-term drug user.

The approach is basically behaviourist – a form of therapy which takes the view that, as drug addiction is a learned behaviour, it can also be unlearned. It offers a combination of therapeutic counselling, group therapy and a daily routine of work and re-education.

Through self-help, self-discovery and self-responsibility, the negative and destructive patterns of behaviour that caused the drug-taking in the first place are addressed and the client's self-esteem and self-confidence are gradually rebuilt until there is no desire to solve problems through taking psychotropic drugs which only harm the body, mind and spirit.

Q Tell me a little more about the 'concept model' of recovery.

The régime at concept model rehabilitation houses is strict and no deviation from the rules is allowed. Usually, no drugs of any kind are allowed. Most residents stay for several months and rehabilitation is carried out in three phases, the first of which lasts for about a month and allows addicts to get used to a drug-free existence.

The second phase tries to get to the heart of the problem – why drug-taking seemed such an attractive solution in the first place. During this phase, the user writes out his or her life history so that attitudes and behavioural patterns can be recognized. The idea behind this is to enable people to see why they might have started taking drugs in the first place.

The third phase prepares former users to socialize with others in a drug-free setting, bearing in mind that they have probably been associating only with other addicts for years. During this phase, clients start thinking about going back to work and re-entering the community as drug-free individuals. They then go out to work but still live in the house.

At first, residents are not allowed family visits – families are so often an integral part of the problem anyway – but, as they move into the third phase, visitors may be received on open days, which are held every 6 weeks or so.

This method of treatment is not suitable for every type of addict – in fact no type of treatment is universally suitable – but is probably most useful to the fairly young user who genuinely wants to make an effort to lead a drug-free life. Many concept houses have a slight Christian flavour, but atheists and non-believers are not turned away.

Some people, but by no means all, experience a spiritual re-awakening at concept houses.

Q What is the most important factor in recovery?

Motivation. The users have to believe, or come to believe, that, if they come off drugs, they will be vastly better off in all respects. Without this motivation, all the support in the world will not be enough, which is why it is impossible to persuade anybody to try and kick a drug habit. Addicts themselves must believe that they can kick the habit, and that they will have a better life afterwards.

Q Are relapses common?

Very. There is no rehabilitation programme in the world which can claim 100 per cent success and drugs are so very powerful in their effects that they can seem a highly seductive means of coping with problems whenever anything goes wrong.

However, addicts should not feel that everything is lost just because they have slid back once or twice. Doctors can be a great help here in reassuring patients that a relapse is not necessarily disastrous. One instance of return to a drug, to which a person was previously heavily addicted, does not inevitably mean he or she is back to square one, although it does indicate how difficult withdrawal can be.

Most experts emphasize that the problem is not so much the physical withdrawal as getting rid of the psychological craving. If addicts do not believe that they are capable of managing the problems for which drugs have always been the sovereign remedy, then they will not think it worthwhile to stop using the drug. For some heavy users, drugs seem to provide the only possible pleasure or escape from an unpleasant world or reality and it can be difficult to persuade such people that life can be better without drugs when they remember how bleak it was before.

This is where rehabilitation houses are invaluable as they attempt to look at the underlying reasons for taking the drugs in the first place and suggest other, better, ways of coping.

Q How important is it to involve the family in recovery?

Most experts consider it is very important indeed because addiction rarely occurs in isolation. There are almost always severe family problems which have brought about, or at least facilitated, the addiction. It is unusual for an addict to come from a completely non-addicted family and most rehabilitation units will involve the family in recovery where possible. In this way, everyone is helped towards an addiction-free life.

Q What are halfway houses?

These are establishments for people who have undergone both detoxification and rehabilitation programmes, but who do not feel capable of conducting themselves independently in the outside world.

Halfway houses are usually converted domestic residences in which former addicts live and work together. Some may already have gained sufficient confidence and ability to take an outside job. Residents are expected to attend a certain number of group therapy sessions – and possibly individual sessions – and to help with the domestic chores. They may share a room or have a room to themselves.

The aim is to prepare long-term users for life in the community and help may be given with obtaining accommodation, jobs and references. The longer a person has been using a drug, the more difficult the transition will be. Those who have succeeded say it is never impossible – and definitely worthwhile.

Q What self-help groups are available?

The best known of the self-help groups for drug users is Narcotics Anonymous (NA), which works on exactly the same lines as all the other 'anonymous' organizations. It is a non-medical, non-drug, self-help society, originally founded about 40 years ago in the USA. The British branch was formed in 1980 in Chelsea, at the time considered the drug centre of London. NA, which has 40–100 people present at every meeting, meets every day of the week.

All its members and organizers are former addicts, or 'cleans'. At each meeting, the organizer – there are no salaries or paid officials – asks for a moment of silence in which members remember why they are there, which is: to stop dying and start living. The Recovery Text, also known as the 'Addicts' Bible', is written proof that the habit can be permanently beaten, according to members.

As with the other Anonymous organizations, the addicts make a promise to themselves to stop taking their drug 'just for today'. A major part of each meeting is taken up with members discussing or sharing their drug problems and what led them to seek recovery. NA members practise complete abstinence from all drugs.

Anyone with a drug problem can go to an NA meeting and their identity will never be revealed. Members are asked to put their belief in a 'higher power', to take a job and to attend NA meetings regularly.

NA's leaflets describe what addiction is not, as they believe this is harder than defining what it is.

According to NA, addiction is not freedom but a habit that soon renders the user incapable of meaningful thought or action. Addiction also serves to isolate the users from other people so that they can exist in their own private world and become incapable of relating to other people. This world is not, however, a pleasant one, but one which is sick, self-centred and self-enclosed.

Drug users who wish to go to rehabilitation houses will often be referred to NA, or asked to attend meetings to strengthen their resolve not to take drugs. Sometimes, attendance at NA meetings is a compulsory requirement before admission to a rehabilitation house.

Q How long would a former user have to attend NA metings?

This depends on how soon the problem is considered to be dealt with. Some people attend meetings several times a week for years, while others feel that a few months is enough. For very many people, though, the road back to permanent abstinence is a hard one, and it takes a lot of help and support before they can be completely confident that the drug habit has been truly overcome.

Q Are there similar meetings that families and relatives can attend?

Yes, Families Anonymous works on similar lines to Al-Anon and Gam-Anon for relatives and family members of alcoholics and gamblers.

FA was started in the belief that families and partners of committed drug users often unwittingly make the problem worse by condemning the habit, hiding substances and making threats, yet at the same time protecting the user from the worst consequences of his or her habit. It is often the case that, if the behaviour towards the drug user of the significant family members can improve, then there is a greater chance of the habit being overcome.

At FA meetings, relatives are taught how to let go of their fears and problems, and are shown how to treat the addict in order to gain the optimum favourable response. Families have to understand that, for the addict, life may become apparently meaningless during recovery.

Deprived of their drug, and yet not established in an alternative, better lifestyle, addicts may become extremely disoriented. They are, above all, people who have ceased to function as autonomous human beings, at least while their lives revolve around getting the next 'fix'.

At FA, it is pointed out that it is often the relatives, rather than the user, who have the most trouble with their emotions and reactions. After all, addicts can blot out their daily worries with their fix. They have found a solution of sorts – the family hasn't.

Anyone can go along to an FA meeting – numbers are in any local phone book – even before the addict in the family has decided to recover. In fact, it is a good idea for close family members who are worried about a relative's drug habit to go along to FA meetings, for advice on what to do for the best and how not to make matters worse.

The amount of courage required to attend NA and FA meetings, because it means admitting the problem at last, should never be underestimated. And problems cannot be solved until they are admitted.

Q Can drug addicts ever become 'normal' people again?

Theoretically, yes. Drug addicts, like alcoholics, are frequently more gifted, more sensitive, more intelligent and creative than average. If they seem morose, anti-social and withdrawn, this is very often as much an effect of the drugs they are taking as their personality. In time, their own personality becomes completely submerged in the drug persona. The problem is that, when the drug is first taken away, there seems to be nothing left but an empty shell. This is why rehabilitation is so important and may, in fact, be essential in order to prepare the former addict for a useful life in the community.

It is often the case that former drug addicts, or addicts in recovery, will find their own way into rehabilitation houses or drug services where they can help others. With drugs, it is always easier to understand what it is like if you have been there yourself.

Q Can former addicts ever have rewarding, intimate relationships?

Eventually, yes. Most agencies recommend that users do not try to form lasting or intimate relationships until they have managed to recover from the drug, bearing in mind that the drug will have become their most intimate friend for the time they have been using.

The close or intimate relationships which people form while they are using drugs are usually with the kind of people known as 'enablers' – those who assist and enable the user to persist in his or her habit, often without fully realizing it. One addict invariably attracts another, and an active addict will always attract an enabler.

When clean all addicts – not just drug addicts – can no longer rely on the mutual attraction between addict and enabler; former users therefore have to discover new ways of relating to others in which the addiction is not part of the attraction. At first, while new types of relationships are set in motion, this may mean loneliness but, as time goes on, and recovery proceeds, most former users find that they become capable of far healthier, friendlier relationships.

No relationship where drugs play an important part can ever be a functional or healthy one. Always, finally, the drug will be more important than the individual. An active addict will lie, steal, cheat, and eventually resort to any kind of criminal behaviour in order to support the habit. The need for constant supplies of the drug will over-ride all human decency. Nobody who wants a good relationship would put up with this kind of behaviour in an intimate companion or partner.

Q Is there any guaranteed way of persuading people not to take drugs in the first place?

Difficult. As we have seen, taking psychotropic drugs is by no means new, and has been practised in every society since the beginning of time, to some extent. It is important to emphasize that only a very small proportion of those who experiment with drugs will become addicts, in much the same way as only a minority of people who drink alcohol will become alcoholics.

Drugs prevention programmes in schools seem to be as successful as anti-smoking programmes, i.e. although they may deter very young people, they have no effect at all on older teenagers. So far, it must be said, no drug prevention programme or advertising campaign, has made the slightest difference to the drugs problem. Just as young people still smoke – in fact, those under 30 years old now represent the largest group of smokers – people are still turning to drugs.

There is probably no guaranteed way to prevent people experimenting with drugs, any more than there is a guaranteed way of preventing them experimenting with sex. What is happening in our society is that pleasures, or vices – however you like to view them – which were once confined to small groups of people, are now being eagerly embraced by all sections of society.

The encouraging news is that there is a wide variety of services now available, run by people who really do understand drug problems and who are taking an increasingly humane approach to the subject. Drug addiction does not have to be a lifetime sentence and there is always a road back to health and sanity for those who wish to avail themselves of it.

One of the great problems with drug addiction is not so much with the individual addict, as the way it affects family members. Also, addicts breed addicts, and, in many cases, drug addiction is deeply embedded in the family history. Almost always, somebody who becomes a drug addict will have come from a family with a multi-generational problem.

Although drug problems cannot always be prevented, they can be successfully treated, and nobody should ever give up hope. Often it is a severe crisis, such as drug addiction, that forces family members to look at and examine their own behaviour so that, through the presenting problem of the addiction, they can find new, better and healthier ways of relating to one another.

Dealing with drug addiction is, for those families who have to face it, a steep and uncomfortable learning curve but, if they are brave enough to go for therapy and treatment together, they can all realize the part they may have played in the situation.

In the words of one former addict:

Deciding to get off the hook – and stay off – could be the single most important thing you ever do in your life, because it is a decision to love and forgive yourself, to put yourself first, to say 'I'm worth it' while allowing yourself all that's empowering and good by living positively in the present. [Corinne Sweet, 1994]

Useful Addresses

Australia

Alcohol and Drug Foundation
(Information, referral, education
and advice)
153 Park Street
South Melbourne
Victoria 3206
Tel: 03 690 6000

Narcotics Anonymous
PO Box 479
Norwood
South Australia 5067
Tel: 08 223 7228

New South Wales Drug and
Alcohol Authority
(All information on research,
drug and alcohol services)
PO Box K700
Haymarket
New South Wales 2000
Tel: 02 217 6666

Palm Lodge Rehabilitation Centre
(In- and out-patient services)
25 David Street
Horsham
Victoria 3400
Tel: 05 382 3113

New Zealand

Community Addiction Services
77 Carrington Road
Auckland
Tel: 860 868

United Kingdom

Angel Project
Tel: 0171 226 3115

Association for the Prevention of
Addiction
37–39 Great Guildford Street
London SE1 0ES
Tel: 0171 620 1919

Broadway Lodge
Totterdown Lane
Off Oldmixon Road
Weston-super-Mare
BS24 9NN
Tel: 01934 812319

City Roads
(24-hour helpline)
356–358 City Road
London EClV 2PY
Tel: 0171 278 8671

Community Drug Project (CDP)
Tel: 0171 703 0559

Families Anonymous
Tel: 0171 731 8060

Institute for the Study of Drug
Dependence (ISDD)
Waterbridge House
32–36 Loman Street
London SE1 0EE
Tel: 0171 928 1211

Lifeline Project
463 Chester Road
Stetford
Manchester M16 9HA
Tel: 0161 848 7227

Mainliners (HIV and AIDS
information)
Tel: 0171 272 4000

Narcotics Anonymous
Tel: 0171 351 6794

Phoenix House (Admissions
Department)
47–49 Borough High Street
London EClN 8ND
Tel: 0181 699 7152

The Priory
Priory Lane
Roehampton
London SW15 5JQ
Tel: 0181 876 8261

Release
(long-established agency with
up-to-date information on all
drugs, rehabilitation houses,
legal matters and recovery)
388 Old Street
London ECl 9LT
Tel: 0171 729 9904

Roma House (Turning Point
project)
67 Talgarth Road
London W14 9DJ
Tel: 0171 603 8383

Standing Conference on Drug
Abuse (SCODA-advice on all
aspects of drug abuse and
information on all drug agencies
and help centres in the UK)
Waterbridge House
32–36 Loman Street
London SEl 0EE
Tel: 0171 928 1211

St Joseph's Centre for Addiction
Holy Cross Hospital
Hindhead Road
Haslemere
Surrey GU27 lNQ
Tel: 01428 656517

Suffolk House
(long-term rehabilitation)
Longbridge
Slough Road
Iver Heath
Bucks SL0 0EB
Tel: 01895 56449

United States of America

Nar-Anon (Family Groups)
PO Box 2562
Palos Verdes, California
90274
Tel: 213 547 5800

Narcotics Anonymous World
Service Office
(This office can put you in touch
with all the major US drug
advice and rehabilitation centres)
PO Box 9999
Van Nuys, California
91409
Tel: 818 780 3951

References

Bethune, H. (1985) Off the Hook – Coping With Addiction.
Methuen.

ISDD (1995) Coping with a Nightmare: Drugs and your Child.

Ives, R. (1991) Soluble Problems. National Children's Bureau.

Judson, H. F. (1968) Heroin Addiction in Britain. Heinemann.

Manning, M. (1985) The Drugs Menace. Columbus.

Parry, A. (1992) The Lancet. Taking Heroin Maintenance Seriously:
The Politics of Tolerance. Vol. 339, February 8, 1992.

Sweet, C. (1994) Off the Hook – How to Break Free from Addiction
and Enjoy a New Way of Life. Piatkus.

Index

Index

Index

psychological addiction 38, 39–40
psychotherapy 26
psychotropic drugs:
    addiction 40
    effects 35–6, 46–7
    prescription 20
purity of drugs 24

Re-Solv 80
recovery 82–104
Recovery Text 95
registered addicts 70–1
rehabilitation 83
rehabilitation centres 77–9, 89–92, 93,
    96–7, 100
relapses 92–3
relationships 100–1
religion 87–8
Ricaurte, Dr George 54–5

schools 64, 102
Seconal 29
self-esteem 66, 90
self-help groups 95–9
sex:
    addiction to 39
    contraception 59
    performance-aiding drugs 34, 51, 57–8
sex hormones 20
Sheffield 90
sinsemilla 28
sleeping pills 20, 30
smack see heroin
smoking 11–12, 19, 47, 65, 102
snow see cocaine
soft drugs 21–3
solvents 17
    effects 34
    long-term effects 56–7
    treatment 79–81
South America 31
speed see amphetamines
spirituality 87–8, 92
Stapleford Centre, London 69
steroids, anabolic 17, 34–5, 42
stimulants 10–11, 17
street agencies 76
sugar 21
suicide 43
Sweet, Corinne 104
symptoms, withdrawal 84–5
synthetic drugs 23–4

taxation 37–8

tea 11, 19, 47
temazepam 33
tetrahydrocannabinoids (THC) 28
tetrazepam 17
tobacco 36, 37, 39
tolerance levels 40
'tough love' 86
tranquillizers 17, 18, 20, 65
    description 33–4
    effects 52
    long-term effects 57
    withdrawal 60
    women users 44
treatment 63–81
    diagnosing drug taking 68–9
    halfway houses 94–5
    hospital clinics 76–7
    instant withdrawal 74–5
    maintenance heroin 71–2, 73–4
    out-patient clinics 78–9
    preventing drug problems 65–7
    registered addicts 70–1
    rehabilitation centres 77–9, 89–92, 93,
        96–7, 100
    signs of drug use 67–8
    solvent users 79–81
    street agencies 76
'trips', LSD 48
Tuinal 29
Twelve Step Minnesota Model 78, 85–9
Tyneside 90

'uppers' see amphetamines; stimulants
urine tests 68
using drugs, definition 18–19

Valium 17
Vietnam War 31

warning signs 67–8
Wirral 90
withdrawal:
    at home 83–5
    clinics 76–8
    heroin 53, 60, 72–4, 84–5
    in hospital 83
    instant 74–5
    relapses 92–3
    symptoms 11, 53, 84–5
women:
    addiction 43–4
    dangers of drug taking 59–61
World War 1 32
World War 2 31